Cute Christmas Vol.2

- COLORING BOOK -

A Christmas Coloring Book for Adults and Kids
Featuring Easy and Relaxing Holiday Scenes with
Cute Animals, Festive Decorations and Much More

an Imprint of **The Fruitful Mind Publishing LTD.**
www.coloringbookcafe.com

Have questions? Let us know.
support@coloringbookcafe.com

 facebook.com/coloringbookcafe

 @coloringbookcafe

This Book
Belongs To:

Santa's House

COLOR CHART

Thank You For Your Purchase

We at Coloring Book Cafe are commited to deliver the best coloring illustrations to our community and we thank you for your support.

Please visit our digital store at:
www.digitalbookcafe.com

Claim your **FREE DIGITAL BOOK** at:
www.freecoloringbooklet.com

Find us on **INSTAGRAM**:
instagram.com/coloringbookcafe

Find us on **FACEBOOK**:
facebook.com/coloringbookcafe

Find us on **AMAZON**:
Search for "Coloring Book Cafe" and find our complete paperback collection on our Amazon Stores in CANADA, USA, AUSTRALIA & The UK

Made in the USA
Monee, IL
24 November 2024